'MY NEW FOREST'

by
ANNETTE MCFARLINE

FOREWORD

ANNETTE McFARLINE was born at Pikes Hill, on the outskirts of Lyndhurst and grew up midst the heather-clad moors and gorse lined bridle paths of the New Forest. A keen walker and pony trekker Annette, through her birthright, is an authority on the New Forest and its history. Widely travelled across the world, it is the New Forest to which she is always happy to return.

Annette nurtures more than just a love of the New Forest. It is, as she herself terms it, a reverence for its landscape and ever-changing moods. The New Forest has served to enhance her natural zest and contentment in life while gaining from the forest's soothing beauty complete peace of mind and solace during times of disharmony and sadness.

An acclaimed writer of poetry, short stories and feature articles, Annette paints a very real picture of the New Forest . . . . . and, if there could possibly be any doubt of its breathtaking beauty, her words are enhanced by full-colour photographs celebrating the natural beauty of some of her favourite New Forest scenes in what must surely be England's loveliest woodland area.

I WONDER

The forest of my childhood
Trickling brooks and bubbling streams
Where ash meets oak and silver birch
A place to build my dreams.

Sunlight dapples the majestic trees
At the dawn of a brand new day
The sky above is azure blue
As here on my back I lay.

Will I be rich and famous
Or travel to foreign lands
Will I shiver in North Alaska
Or lay upon sunkissed sands?

Will I journey to India or China
Hong Kong or Timaru
Will I see the Taj Mahal in moonlight
Or stay in Katmandu?

Will I sail upon the open seas
Or fly the starry skies
Will I stroll upon the desert wastes
Climb snowy mountains way up high?

This land of trees and flowers
Of heather moors and gorse-filled bowers
Of ponies grazing wild and free
This is the place I'd rather be.

COME WITH ME

Come with me through purple heather
Come with me through stormy weather
Come to where the streams run free
If you dare – then come with me.

Come to where the ponies graze
Hold my hand – don't be afraid
Come and see where flowers bloom
In the heat of day at noon.

Come with me through sun and shade
Rest yourself in a leafy glade
Come and see where deer will feed
Where beauty reigns with God indeed.

Come and see where bluebells grow
Where gorse is golden and rivers flow
Whisper not – don't make a sound
For surely this is Holy Ground.

SPARKLING DAYS

Frost and ice . . . . then let us go
With cheeks aflame and hearts aglow
To trudge and trek the white-washed ways
Climb high the hills on winter days.

The ponies do not share our fun
Cowered together – they become as one
With winter coats to keep them warm
Unlike the stags and doe or tiny fawn.

If Jack Frost bites the streams will freeze
Trees will stand naked, devoid of leaves
The forest floors as hard as rock
While sheep will huddle within their flocks.

Water frozen in icy fingers
As creatures scuttle afraid to linger
Puddles settle like polished glass
While pointed needles replace the grass.

The forest resembling a well-iced cake
All covered in snow as we awake
With eyes so round, mouths set in awe
So overwhelming – Mother Nature's law.

The snowy scene with more to come
Signals that we'll have lots of fun
The moorland is a desert land
With clean pure snow instead of sand.

Our footprints trample across the snow
As hither and thither thus we go
A snowman to build or a snowball fight
Such laughter in this world of white.

IN THE WINTER SNOW

The Forest paths are lost from sight
As heath and heather dressed in virgin white
Are as a bride waiting for her groom
So faraway is the warmth of June.

The snow so deep upon the ground
Shows all footprints – muffles most sounds
The still cold nights and crisp clear days
Nowhere near is the warmth of May.

Oaks and ash are bathed in lightness
The forest floodlit in a heavenly brightness
While little robins fly cold skies
These birds unseen in a hot July.

So still, so silent, so ethereal
The world looks pure and heaven seems real
This land where saints and kings have trod
This place of beauty that belongs to God.

IN FOREST MIST

The Forest shrouded in an opal mist brings forth a host of thoughts
Of half-forgotten memories and ambitions once we sought
Of once beloved people we no longer bring to mind
While shattered dreams and promises are never far behind.

The air is dank upon our face as through the mist we walk
And leaves droop listless on the boughs as beside us memory stalks
Time stands as still as stone on the chilly threatening air
While the past becomes the present and we are haunted here by care.

Problems and hurts of long ago with us play hide and seek
As mist and fog dull our brains and to our senses seep
All reasoning and common sense completely desert us now
As heart and mind dissolve as one in the white impenetrable cloud.

Why then this trip into the past – why walk in forest fogs
Why venture out in damp and mist to skirt the heathland bogs
What point is there in looking aft and revisiting ancient pains
Why turn around and journey back once more down Memory Lane.

But it was not planned, I'd no idea, that the mist would close in on me
I did not know, it came so fast, like a storm upon the sea
The fog that would bar my way and mirror the past to face
So thick the fog, so white the mist, there seems just no escape.

Yet to face the past and learn from it is surely wisdom indeed
It's a foolish man who makes mistakes and refuses then to heed
Much more is learned from harder times than ever from happy hours
As a garden is weeded with thought and care – to produce the brightest flowers.

So perhaps every now and then we should stand still and take stock
Think about the track of by-gone years, the memories to unlock
Music may trigger the flow of thought or old photographs lead the way.....
There's always something in everyone's life and for me it's a misty day.

But I'll turn my footsteps homeward now and make my gentle way
And every footstep that I tread will keep the past at bay
I'll make the present as happy as I can and harbour no lowly ways
So that when the present becomes the past there'll be sunshine on misty days.

LENGTHENING DAYS

One minute a night since the shortest day
The light unfolds and with it brings
A sense of expectancy, a touch of magic
As we anticipate the arrival of Spring.
Pussy willows appear from nowhere
As strong little heads pop through the soil
The promise of things to come is with us
The whisper of Spring to one and all.
Primrose heads and daffodil noses
Snowdrops, crocus and tulip tips
Bluebells green but thick as cabbages
Grateful prayers upon our lips.

SPRING'S ARRIVAL

Amid the greys and beige of winter's hold
The first splashes of Spring appear
Snowdrops glistening white, crocuses of gold and violet
Dance in their splendour upon the air.

The trees are heavy with voluptuous buds
And daffodils grow tall and strong
While the first pink blossoms are here at last
As blackbird warbles his Springtime song.

Through the muddied brown of winter
Springtime colours burst through the gloom
Pinks and lemons, golds and lilacs
Emerge from Mother Nature's womb.

MY NEW FOREST PRAYER

Golden leaves or Spring time flowers
Summer heat or snowfilled showers
Skies of blue or skies of grey
In this Forest may I stay.

Let me walk the Forest ways
There to spend all of my days
Paths that take me high and low
Where trees are tall and rivers flow.

Through inclosures, over heather
Across the fields in stormy weather
Climbing trees and running free
Oh what happiness here for me.

FROM LITTLE ACORNS

Being under oak trees
Is like being with old friends
They reach out and comfort us
A soothing love they send
Mighty oak trees tall and strong
With arms outstretched
Safe, sure and long.

Under oak trees may I pray
In the cool of an evening
Or the warmth of a day
The rustling leaves and gnarled wood
Chase cares away .....
Turn bad to good.

FAR AND WIDE

From Colbury's Church to Deer Leap
From Pook's Green to Bucklers Hard
Such views to soften the toughest heart
I'll wager a winning hand of cards.

From Hatchet Pond to Mogshade Hill
From Stoney Cross to Fordingbridge
The heather lands stretch wide and free ...
While Copythorne leads on to Ridge.

Blackbush to Eyeworth to Holiday's Hill
Emery Down to Bolton's Bench to Long Down
The forest's mystery and beauty ever present ...
A heaven on earth is found.

From Mockbeggar to Milkham to Acres Down
Here ponies love to roam
In seasons of chill and in seasons of gold
This beautiful land is home.

NEW FOREST SONG

The New Forest gives me inexplicable pleasure
It's highways and byways I always shall treasure
It's heather clad moors, it's gorse and it's ponies
It's inclosures where I have never been lonely.
To breathe the air and smell the wood
To catch the seasons change the Forest's mood
What heaven is this in an uncertain world
To witness the Forest – it's beauty unfurled.

CHRISTMAS TIME

Does the Forest know it's Christmas
Do birds and animals understand the time ....
Have a party – visit each other
Prepare a meal or have some wine ....

Can you imagine little creatures
Say Mr. Field-Mouse in bow tie and suit
Mrs. Squirrel in a brand new petticoat
While Mr. Hare gets out his flute.

There would be dancing in the rabbit holes
And singing high in the trees
Ponies nuzzle 'Goodwill to All Men'
While bunnies try so hard to please.

Is there a place where they like to meet
All the animals on Christmas Morning
Do mice wear surplices to sing carols
As the break of day is dawning.

Whatever happens in the forest
It is important for all of us to remember
That it's Christmas time for Everything
And animals too have their twenty-fifth December.

MY PRAYER

When I smile at the sky, Lord,
It is my way of thanking you
For all the things you've given me
For blessings rich and true
And one day I pray you will show me
What I can do for you ....

SLUFTERS

Across the moors on sandy track
Through trees and gorse lined vales
The path way winds and twists and turns
Midst bushes, shrubs and prickly ferns...
The path snakes down to copse then on to purple heather
Views of beauty stretch to right and left as we ride and talk together
The crunch of hoof, the smell of sap, the feel of softened leather
And on and on the pathway leads .... to Burley's Outer Rails
As we trot merrily on our way to the gate, where we dismount
    and lean
To stand and stare and breathe this air so clean ...
The horses graze, girths loosened, while we survey the way
    we've come
Our gaze then travelling to the gate where someone has engraved ...
A forester, a rider, a walker, someone before us has stood as
    we stand
And that person has written our private thoughts ...
'For All This Beauty Belongs to God.'

MY NEW FOREST ALMANAC

Fireworks blaze and bonfires crackle
Apples bob and witches cackle
Woodsmoke hanging on the air
And Foxes scamper to their lair.

Walk in the Forest in bleak November
Only joy can come remember
The golden colours all around
Proclaim that here is heavenly ground.

Ponies with their new coats growing
Stand amidst the colours glowing
Crunching leaves under feet
Where Oak and Ash and Beech trees meet.

December comes with Christmas nigh
And thoughts of Santa Clause come by
Frosts are sharp and mornings cold
A tradition that is ever old.

Cottages with chimneys smoking
A sudden shower and we are soaking
But still we pray with all our might
Please let this Christmas be all white.

Christmas Day with church bells ringing
Choirs of angels singing ... singing
Little snowflakes start to fall
"Merry Christmas" and good luck to all.

Boxing Day and the Hunt is out
Red fox is keeping low his snout
Beagles bark and huntsmen sound
Proclaiming this is hunting ground.

January and the year is new
The New Forest wakes to me and you
We face the year with faith and hope
Our futures clean as washed in soap.

The trees are bare, the ground is firm
The Forest is in its winter term
Animals are safe and warm inside
It is only we who stay outside.

With faces red and cheeks all tingling
We with the cattle keep our mingling
Woollen scarves and hats on heads
Those lucky creatures in their beds!

But soon the birds will start to sing
The Forest looks forward to the Spring
Snowdrops bursting all around
As Mr. Mole stirs underground.

February arrives and lovers tarry
Many plan that soon they'll marry
Carving initials on a tree
A boy for you, a girl for me.

Crocuses and violets showing
St. Valentines Day and all are knowing
That pussy willows grace the trees
And boats are lost on stormy seas.

Spring time lamb and little bunny
Chocolate eggs ooze cream and honey
Daffodil scents fill the air
And new foal nuzzles close his mare.

Primroses carpet Fairy Wood
I wouldn't pick them if I could
Blossoms heavy on the trees
Thank you Lord for all of these.

The air is warm and truly mellow
Mr. Cuckoo sings his 'hello'
Bluebells peep at every turn
Jostling with the light green fern.

Rhododendrons line the Rhinefield Drive
Where scented azaleas seem to thrive
We say farewell to April showers
And welcome all these Maytime flowers.

Rooks build high their nests in trees
Old friends return from overseas
The sun grows stronger all the while
And Mother Nature lends her smile.

Sunlight kisses ferns and heather
As we enjoy this glorious weather
The sun more evident than the moon
Oh lovely month – this month of June.

Strawberries red with cream so white
Days so long with warm short nights
The farmers start to make the hay
July will follow – come what may.

So the Forest in month of seven
Reflects its beauty as part of heaven
Ponies doze and blink their eyes
Flicking tails in defence of flies.

Buckets and spades and sandy beaches
Long cool drinks, ice cream with peaches
Rolling seas and a quiet bay
Our thoughts take wing to a holiday.

Bournemouth, Highcliffe, the Isle of Wight
The choice is wide and our plans take flight
We may plunge ourselves or choose to paddle
Shed our shoes and clothes, ponies their saddles.

But back to the Forest in September shine
Where living continues rich and fine
The mornings cool and as clear as wine
With fragrant days of sap and pine.

Silver cobwebs on the hedgerows
And the winds begin to blow...
Shorter days and early night fold
Leaves and ferns turn to russet and gold.

All God's creatures start to scurry
Squirrels with nuts in such a hurry
Guy Fawkes Night is here again
Another year has passed my friend.

HEDGEROWS

Lord may I show my love
In my life of every day
May I make it somehow easier
For fellow travellers on their way
As hedgerows glisten after showers of rain
May I share your ears to listen
To ease another's pain.

MOGSHADE HILL

High on the moorland from Emery Down
Where today the trippers stop for their picnics
There stands a simple rugged cross of wood
Erected as a monument to peace and good.

American and Canadian soldiers were stationed in the New Forest
And far away from their families and native homes
They found this place so reminiscent of their motherland
So carved their monument with wood to hand.

The cross with a small garden surround
Looks down upon a scene of breathtaking loveliness
Such a vista of fir trees of outstanding beauty
Homesick soldiers erected the cross as part of their duty.

And to this day at the 11th hour on the 11th day of the 11th month
A Sunday Service of Remembrance is celebrated at the Cross
New generations stand in the chill air of November
As with bowed heads they in turn remember ..... loved ones lost.

The Last Post is sounded and soars over the trees
As the people of today recall heroes of yesteryear
The men and boys who found comfort here
Whose hearts were lonely and for eyes that shed no tears.

For those who returned home the assembled company will give
    thanks
For those who did not .... there is sadness and remembrance
For those soldiers hurt or wounded or dead
On Mogshade Hill, at the foot of the Cross, there remains a wreath of
    red ....

AT TWILIGHT TIME

Twilight time in Fairy Wood
Is a place to stroll and dream
To watch the sky silhouette the trees
And listen to gurgling streams.

At twilight time in Fairy Wood
You can hear the squirrels play
And clap your hands to the dancing ferns
At the close of every day.

At twilight time in Fairy Wood
Mr. Owl wakes up from sleep
With night time friends he greets the dark
His watch in turn to keep.

At twilight time in Fairy Wood
Creatures tumble one and all
To chase each other among the trees
And scamper on to the moor.

At twilight time in Fairy Wood
Elfins whisper in bunny ears
And pixies play with friendly voles
While gnomes play tag with deer.

At twilight time in Fairy Wood
Forest friends begin to scurry
Some to make their way to bed
Others the night to hurry.

At twilight time in Fairy Wood
The bats prepare to fly
They greet the night with happy relief
Wings stretched towards the sky.

At twilight time in Fairy Wood
Mr. Fox departs his lair
Through the woods he stealthily prowls...
The Forest's Millionaire.

At twilight time in Fairy Wood
It's wise to leave at close of day
Allow the creatures to have their fun ...
And they will frolic the night away.

THE DRIPPING FOREST

To walk in the forest in drizzling rain
Does much to ease the soul of pain
To be among trees in anguish and sorrow
Will soothe away hurt and maybe tomorrow ...
Things will look brighter and not quite so bleak
We will feel stronger – not anxious or weak.

Walking uphill and down forest slope
Trust you'll be better and able to cope
Watching the ponies stand side by side
They'll listen to problems you may confide
Remember no answers can they give
For ponies too have to manage and live.

So on we walk still lost in thought
Surely here's the answer to that we sought
For standing still and letting be
Is doubtless the answer – for can't you see
That putting your faith in the good Lord above
His hand will guide you in faith and with love.

Not flowers fair at every turn
This is a lesson we must learn
Sunny skies not always there
But rainy ones – with many cares
Our paths not easy and smooth to walk
But rough and treacherous where danger stalks.

The winds may blow and the rain may lash
The trees may tremble and the thunder crash
But God is there always by our side
No harm will come on Life's ebb tide
To walk with Him always hand in hand
Will make this Forest Our Promised Land.

ROMANY HOME

Gone this day the Lord has ordained
Darkness comes as the shadows fall
Trees like soldiers stand to attention
Obeying Mother Nature's law.

At King's Garden all is quiet
Not a murmur amongst the trees
All is silent – without movement
No gentle rustling of the leaves.

Darkness is falling deep and long
And the woods are covered by an inky sky
Like a black velvet curtain it closes in
As the night draws slowly nigh.

Not for me a fire and hearth
Not for me a house and home
The Forest is my mansion house
Here no need for brush or comb.

It can be cold sometimes, my friend,
And I've shivered in clothes which were damp
But there's nothing like a hot bowl of soup
By a fire in a gypsy camp.

The sky is the roof of my world
While the stars will watch over me
The moon's the only chimney I'll possess
And, you know, the rent is free.

I know every sound the Forest makes
And here I am safe and secure
No dangers lurk for a gypsy soul
And the city has no allure.

I tried the city once, you know,
But that life was not for me ...
Why, I missed the grass and gorse and ferns
And all of my friends ... the trees.

You may frown at a gypsy's life
Good for nothing some would say
But I am rich for I'm healthy and strong
And I thank God every day...

I thank Him for my happy life
Which is purely a matter of choice
I thank Him for the heather and moors
With a loud and joyful voice.

I thank Him for the sky above
And praise Him for the sun and shade
For dappled glades and babbling brooks
For all the creatures He has made.

For all God's riches in the Forest
I thank him loud and long
For the sunshine warm upon my back ...
His presence that makes me strong.

LINKS WITH THE PAST

Beaulieu Road means pony sales
While Lymington Sound means billowing sails
Keyhaven with reminders of ancient battles
Fritham .... the stable of families of cattle.
Rich in trees and a wealth of plenty ....
Are the woods of Boldre and Denny
Memories return of wars once fought ....
Sopley, Blackbush and Moyles Court.
Calshot, Lepe and Beaulieu Estuary ....
Today the tourists enjoy to ferry
While sea gulls wheel and cry the skies
Where here scullduggery in disguise.

Gracious houses where ghosts will stalk
Could tell such tales if walls could talk
Of illicit meetings and assignations
Which even today could cause sensation.
A hunting lodge owned by Nell Gwynn –
A gift to her from a well-loved King
One can picture them strolling in the grounds
His lace cravat .... her embroidered gown.
'A' roads and 'B' roads of concrete and bitumen
Were once unmade and ridden by highwaymen
And still today a coach and four in flight
Haunts the road to Brook on a moonless night.

HOLLY HATCH

When far away from my New Forest home
My thoughts will always return
Where the ground is purple and the skies are blue
Fresh green are the trees, old gold are the ferns.

When over seas and my mood is pensive
The expression on my face is easy to catch
For I am dreaming of a path which forks on a distant moor
Where one path runs to the Bluebell Wood....the other to Holly Hatch.

Over the brow of the hill and there it is below
A scene of sweet comfort and delightful harmony
Where cool clear waters bubble and flow
And life is as tranquil as a calm upon the sea.

Cities and towns and foreign markets
Noise and bustle forming a hectic match
Crowds of people of jostling nations ....
Send me back to Holly Hatch.

NOT MINE ALONE

I say 'My Forest' but it's not mine alone
I wish it were ... as it is my home
It is my treasure and my bounty
The shining jewel of Hampshire County.

I need the Forest as I need to breathe
Every inclosure and moor - I will not leave
Here for me my church and chapel
Amongst the trees and glades sun dappled.

Brockenhurst to Burley to Holidays Hill
I will never, of course, exhaust my fill
Minstead to Ringwood, on to Crow Hollow
'Mid purple heather, bridle paths to follow.

Fordingbridge to Black Bush to Acres Down
If I had troubles, well, here they'd drown
Lymington to Keyhaven and back to Boldre
A love that strengthens as I grow older.

MY FOREST

When your way is rough and steep
Why not to my Forest creep
Bridle paths and picturesque moors
Soft and sandy moss-clad floors.

When your way is hard to climb
Come to my Forest to ease your mind
Walk in thought on tracks of gravel
There your worries to unravel.

Too many problems on your plate?
Why not lean on Heaven's Gate
Watch the sun move through the trees
Feel your troubles start to ease.

MY LAST WILL & TESTAMENT

As with the sun my spirit sinks slowly in the west
Carry me to the place I love the best
Not to some remembrance garden of peace and good
Rather to a place I love – called Denny Wood.

Let the New Forest floor be my final resting place
So that my spirit may wander immortal in time and space
Where the trees meet in cathedral arches
Stately oaks and elms and coniferous larches.

No mournful singing in a sombre church
But hymns of praise beneath a silver birch
For this forest that I have happily trod
This for me is the House of God.

Scatter my ashes at the break of dawn
My soul to wing with doe and fawn
My spirit to soar with the birds above
To live here forever in beauty and love.

When I pass through that heavenly door
You'll still feel my presence on Beaulieu Moor
You'll see me reflected in a dappled glade
So you're not to worry – or be afraid.

You'll hear me down at Pixies Nook
So stop and listen as you pass the brook
Hear me whisper to you through the trees
I'll never leave you – so please don't grieve.

In Spring I'll dance with the flowers new
You'll smell my perfume amid bells of blue
In Summer heat I'll fly with the bumble bees
As your prayers you say upon your knees.

When Autumn kisses the forest with gold
Then my colours too I will unfold
Soon will come the season to be merry
Ice cold days and holly berry.

The forest now in winter snow
I shall still walk – but no footsteps show
The ground is hard and glitters bright
As I stroll the forest dressed in white.

The years will come and the years will go
My spirit will linger and glide and flow
With Mother Nature I'll be maternal
My soul and spirit here – eternal.